ONE GIRL'S SEARCH
FOR HOPE

ONE GIRL'S SEARCH FOR HOPE

Revised Edition

KATHRYN HOOVER

Table of Contents

Part 1..4
Part 2..8
Part 3..12
Part 4..19
Part 5..23
Part 6..26
Part 7..29
Part 8..33
Part 9..37
Part 10..42
Part 11..46
Part 12..50
Part 13..55
Part 14..59
Part 15..63
Part 16..68
Part 17..72
Part 18..77
Part 19..81
Contact info..87

Part 1

On April 29, 1989 a tiny preemie girl was born in Rochester, NY to Mennonite parents at 11 weeks early. She was very tiny, weighing 1 lb. 9.5 oz. and measuring 12.25 inches long. Most of her time she spent in an incubator as at that time her mom was only allowed to hold her for half an hour each day. At 4 weeks of age she got very sick and the doctors didn't know what was wrong and gave her every medication they could think of trying to stop this unknown illness.

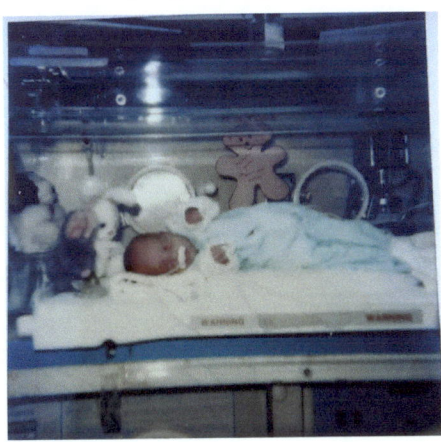

Finally they realized it was spinal meningitis which could be fatal if not caught in time. Most who have this disease often end up with disabilities caused by the disease but she was blessed to survive with none of the after effects which could have been asthma or deafness, etc. She got to go home for the first time when she was 10 weeks old.

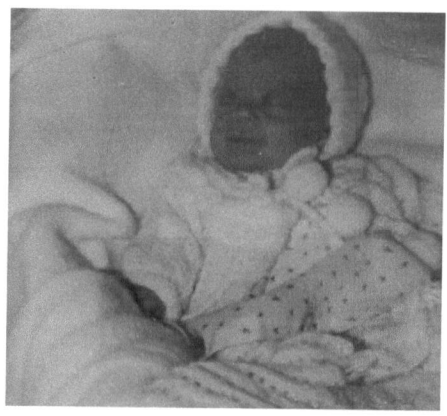

She had a childhood just like any other child, being taught right from wrong and siblings being added to the family. But there were a few things that weren't right about her family. Every morning after breakfast the family would read a chapter out of the Bible which was good but as she grew older and began to understand things she realized that even though her parents read the Bible and told her how she should do, they did the opposite causing much confusion. She didn't feel loved. Instead there was always work to be done and she never knew when her dad would get angry and hit her for something she didn't do right or sometimes wasn't even her fault. She had to find a way to cope with all the stress and it showed up in school. She was home-schooled until 5th grade, then she went to a private school which only added to the stress. She had a very hard time focusing on her lessons, every day taking home nearly every book assigned that day, unfinished. Mocking by some of the older students compounded the problem. As she continued to bring books home, the punishments also grew. She had to skip meals or dessert as punishment, often going to bed after 11:00 at night because she couldn't focus, often ending in spankings for not getting her assignments done. One such night dad took her and her sister outside to punish them. By then she understood enough of the Bible that she knew there was a God and that the Bible said He was loving and kind but she wondered what love and kindness meant. They were only words to her. As she stood on the porch waiting for the punishment she looked up into the clear starlit sky. A wordless plea to this God that was supposed to be real rose from her heart, but in that moment as the punishment fell she felt like God turned his back on her as though He didn't care.

Another way she dealt with the stress was to go out in the woods and watch the birds. She was too scared to go far into the woods because she had heard too many bad stories of wild animals. One such time she was sitting on a little tuft of grass that jutted out into the middle of the creek that meandered through the meadow. As she sat there trying to find comfort for her troubled soul in the babbling of the brook and staying out of sight, she looked up to the cloudy sky and tried to talk to the God that the Bible said is real. She wanted to feel Him. She wanted peace. She wanted love.

As she got older she started reading mystery books and then incorporated some of the techniques into a new way of dealing with the stress; by making a game out of trying to outsmart her dad. Because all the homework caused late nights, it made it very hard to get out of bed the next morning. The only thing that kept her going was the fear of what her dad would do if she wasn't fast enough to get up and out to the barn in time to help with the chores. She soon learned that if she didn't get out fast enough and saw dad coming she had a way of escaping by slipping out another door and having different ways of getting around dad without him knowing. There were times when she could have reached out and touched dad from where she was hiding and he had no idea that she was there. At least 2 times he caught her and it was almost impossible to keep from panicking because she saw how he beat the animals when they didn't obey and she feared for her life, which caused her and her sister to one day start digging a cave on the gully bank which stopped when dad found his pick ax lying close by.

Part 2

After she graduated from 8th grade she didn't know what lay ahead for her except to stay at home to help with the work in the middle of the dysfunctionality of her home life which looked very bleak and lifeless. All she saw was that she was expected to help with the work, go out on cleaning jobs as her mom set them up, and not looking forward to turning 16 when she was expected to go with the other youth to the gatherings where they would spend an hour or 2 singing and then 2 hrs of volleyball or some other activity till it was time to go home. As she was mocked in school so she expected to get mocked by those same people when she joined the youth group.

One day after she graduated she and her sister were in the shop doing something when dad came storming angrily into the shop demanding of them where they put his vise grip. They didn't know where it was but they also knew that their dad had a habit of not keeping his tools in the right place and so when he needed them later he couldn't find them. She quickly started looking for it as hard as she could all the while trying to keep her distance from dad because it was hard telling what he would do if she got close enough. Finally he gave up looking and went off again and she slipped out behind the barn in a secluded spot and burst into sobs, her heart shattered. As she wept she looked up into the clear blue sky with bright sun and begged God to send some angels to take her out of this hell of a life! She had no hope. No dreams. No peace for her troubled soul. No desire to live anymore.

There was a Bible course by mail that her mom did as a young girl and she wanted her children to do it. So she set it up and got them started. When this girl was about 16 years old she was doing her mailbox club lesson one day and it talked about salvation and how it is asking Jesus to come into her heart and she will feel different. At the end of the lesson there was a short prayer to pray if she wanted to be saved. A glimmer of hope rose in her battered heart. She wanted something different. She wanted to feel better. She wanted hope. She found a quiet spot and sincerely prayed that prayer expecting to feel different. But she was disappointed. As time went on she didn't feel any different. Instead she wondered if she didn't pray the prayer the right way. In the course of the next few years, she prayed that prayer several times, never feeling a change. She was discouraged. What she didn't realize though was that God had heard her prayer and saw her sincere desire and He was working in a very gentle way as only He can in a shattered heart. First she realized that it was wrong for her to go off to a secluded place with her cousins at family gatherings and tell dirty jokes and stories. When she realized it, the next time that they were together, she found a book to read and curled up by the bookshelf and read the afternoon away; but not without consequences, for when one of her cousins found her later he mocked her for it.

She also realized that the filthy books she read while at her cleaning jobs were filling her mind with pornographic images and she no longer found excitement in them, so she chose to no longer read them despite the temptation that awaited her every time. But God was ready and filled that void with something else: a hunger for Him which caused her to read the Word and search for Him in the Scriptures. Soon her favorite book became Isaiah. She also started memorizing Scriptures while doing chores to help curb the filthy images in her mind from all the filthy books she had read. She also began to desire a better life. She wanted an example to follow but could find none. Instead she felt trapped. She didn't know what to do and because of that, the hopelessness grew greater than ever because she felt there was no way out. She wanted to end it all; yet God had a plan.

Part 3

The usual age for the youth to get baptized in that church is 17 and older so when her friends in the youth brought up the subject she agreed because she sincerely wanted to be baptized because she believed. So that summer found her in instruction class getting instructed in the 18 articles of faith used in the church as a foundation for the beliefs. In the fall she was sprinkled with water with the rest of her friends in a "baptism" ceremony. She was then considered a member of that church. The two were considered inseparable. She joined that church because she did not know where else to go. Any other church was considered more liberal and worldly and leaving the church was considered bad no matter what the reason was. But in her heart she wondered if this is all or is there more? When she read about Jesus doing miracles she wondered why the only miracles she hears of are in books? When she would read about the baptism of the Holy Ghost with the evidence of speaking in other tongues in Acts she wondered if it's still real today or if it really is in the past and was only for the first disciples like the church leaders said. She also had lots of questions about the church rules and why the church did things the way they did. But she suppressed the questions because she had no one she trusted enough to ask.

As life went on the hopelessness and suicidal thoughts grew greater. In the fall after she turned 18 she was asked to teach school.

She did like to study and to her it looked like a way to get away from home so she said yes. Every day she had a driver that took her and her co-teacher the 9 miles back and forth to school. She was now the teacher of grades 3-6 with around 15 students and enjoyed watching their faces light up when they grasped a new concept. By now there was so much pain and hurt in her heart that the only way to cope with it was to try to block her feelings so she didn't feel anything(which she had already been doing for years. Numbness was normal.). It also affected her appetite. She hardly ate anything. Even when she came home from school at suppertime she only ate a spoonful or two until the constant fuss and bickering of her siblings and parents overwhelmed her and she went to her room to get away. At the end of the term she was quite surprised when her co-teacher informed her that she would not be teaching the next year because she felt like all the responsibility of discipline lay on her shoulders. She was surprised because she thought she had been doing her part. She was determined to try harder next year.

The next year another friend agreed to be her co-teacher but she wanted grades 1-3. So the switch was made and now instead of 3-6th grade she had grades 4-8. It all seemed to be going well until one day in October of 2008 she brought her journal to school for her co-teacher to read and left it on her desk after she left for the day not expecting anyone to come. What she didn't know was that her 4th grade girl brought some stuff to school(her parents were on the board) after she was gone and read her journal. It then bothered her so much she told her parents.

The next evening she came home to only find her parents in the house and the children were all outside which was rather unusual. As she went over to the desk to see if anything interesting came in the mail, mom who looked like she had been crying, came over to her and asked if she ever felt suicidal.

"Yes," she said.

Then they took her into their bedroom for privacy and asked why she felt that way. She told them it's because dad's always angry. She was not able to really say more than that but she noticed her dad wipe away a tear which she had never seen before. Apparently he actually cared, she thought. They told her that the school board no longer wants her at school and another of her friends will be finishing the term for her. So that next week she found herself headed to PA with family to take her for an evaluation at Green Pastures/Philhaven clinic. They asked her questions, looked at her journals full of scribbles and talked with her parents. They decided to put her in Green Pastures which is a Mennonite and Amish-run place for the mentally ill. They almost put her in Philhaven because of the suicidal tendencies which was a hospital facility for mentally ill patients. Since there was no opening till Thursday, she went to stay with her maternal grandparents till there was room for her.

After she was given her room at Green Pastures she climbed into the bed. Now and then one of the mentors would check up on her and to ask her how she was. She would sit on the edge of the bed and talk to her. The mentor's voice was always kind and her touch gentle. She didn't know how to handle all this kindness. She had been used to harsh words and bickering siblings and arguing parents. It began to overwhelm her.

On Sunday an Amish preacher came with some more Amish families to have church with the residents. He preached on love and as this girl sat next to the mentor and listened to the kind words of the man rise and fall in her ears she started to cry and couldn't stop. Finally she asked the mentor if she could go to the restroom and when given permission she went and sat on the floor and wept. She was realizing that she believed that there weren't any kind people left in the world anymore. All the kindness was cracking her walls of self-protection.

After a bit the mentor knocked on the door asking for entrance. As the girl unlocked the door the mentor came in and just held her close in her arms for a while till she could control herself and then asked her what was wrong. After an explanation the mentor took her to her room where she stayed most of the rest of the day, crying. It was a moment when God used the kindness of others to unearth a deeply embedded lie in this girl's life. Then began the journey of trust and learning to deal with feelings. It took a while to even start getting better.

After 10 weeks she was released and went to live with relatives because they wouldn't let her go home yet but she did after 3 months because she was homesick for the poisonous atmosphere she grew up in because that's what she was used to.

She was home for a few months but she felt like what she really needed was counseling so she went to a home for girls to get counseling. It was the beginning of a long journey and after 4 months the homesickness again became too much so she went back home.

She began working for her aunt and in Jan. 2010 her aunt took her to a seminar for Truehope promoting a natural pill supplement for people diagnosed bipolar. Her aunt told her that if the girl is interested she will buy the first bottle for her. She agreed because the 4 drugs she was on made her feel doped and it was worth a try anyway. It went well.

Soon she wanted more counseling so in August she went to her great-uncle, who was a bishop in the church, and they worked through John Regier's book Biblical Concepts of Counseling, asking forgiveness for and renouncing strongholds the enemy had through occultic practices, generational sins, and other areas. There was definitely more freedom and healing in her life. Hope was beginning to creep into her heart.

Part 4

She then started realizing that her parents' home has a poisonous atmosphere and if she wants more healing she needs to leave. So in an effort to break the ties and feeling that her parents wouldn't just give her the liberty to move out, she saw an ad in Die Botschaft, a Mennonite and Amish newspaper, and took the opportunity to move 5 hrs away to a new community to teach the 8 school-age children. She lived in a mobile home on one of the school parents' property and had the schoolroom set up in her living room. It went ok even though she was starting to feel emotions she didn't know how to deal with.

There were times when in the evening she would see the husband walking to the house after chores were done and the loneliness would overwhelm her and she would cry. The atmosphere in their home was different from what she grew up in and now that some healing had taken place she yearned to be in a better atmosphere. Even though she missed her youngest siblings she no longer missed the atmosphere.

She had a 7th grader that was very hard to deal with and just the stress of all the change etc. broke her down till she was sick in bed. After a week or 2 the school parents decided she should go to the one family's house because she was too sick to be alone, which ended up being at the 7th grader's house, the very one that was causing most of the stress. Towards the end of the term she was asked if she'd teach again. She agreed, not knowing where else to go as she certainly didn't want to go home again.

In the last week or 2 of school she realized that she will not be emotionally able to handle it and with a friend's help found a place to live in PA and a maid job for the summer. She moved in with a widow lady who had a Boston Terrier. It was a playful puppy and the girl was warned that she may not hit the dog because it will make her nasty. So with that warning and her timidness she was afraid of the dog. The maid job went well but the living situation did not. The dog seemed to realized that she could do what she wanted. She would jump up and bite the girl in the middle of the back or on the arm. It was even worse when the widow lady's daughter came over with her Boston Terrier.

Because of the girl's shyness and mistrust of people she didn't talk much but stuck to her room or the basement where she had a corner for her projects. This caused the widow lady to fuss because the girl didn't trust her enough to share the things bothering her and when she did try she wasn't respected and listened to so she just shut herself up in her room spending time reading and talking to God.

In the fall when the maid job was over she found a job at a fabric store.

One day the widow lady went to a funeral in NY and met a lady that told her that this girl was diagnosed bipolar and should be on medication. This girl, knowing the diagnosis, had studied up on Bipolar just a little bit beforehand and believed it to be a misdiagnosis. The widow lady came back from her trip all fired up and when she couldn't get much out of the girl she went to talk with her friends at church about it. It got worse and worse till the friend who had helped her find the place in the beginning, came to visit and told her that in order to quench the fire of gossip that has been started, she should go for a second evaluation. The friend was planning to go with her and was staying with her.

One evening 2 days before the scheduled appointment, the widow told the girl she needs to move. The girl was not really surprised and she had been trying to find another place to live for the last 2 weeks and still be able to keep her job with no success. Nobody wanted her. She felt like she had just been thrown on the street without any place to go. So with her friend's help she got everything packed up the next day and then went to her friend's sister's place for the night.

Part 5

The next morning was the appointment. The girl and her friend went with her counselor to the appointment. The doctor confirmed that it had been a misdiagnosis only suggesting something for sleep since the girl was not sleeping well because of all the stress. She was also told that Sunlight Gardens, which had just opened as a halfway house for "plain" girls in transition from Philhaven to their home community, was expecting her.

They went over there and after looking around she asked if she could stay because she had nowhere else to go. They accepted her.

Now began another stage of the healing process. The creativity inside the girl's brain began to reveal itself. It showed up on the walls, in the flowerbeds, and in many different ways all around the place. But as the creativity came out, so also did the anger that had been stored inside all of her childhood that she had never dared to really show before. The mentors knew that if the girl wasn't around she was probably sitting up on the attic stairs because the anger was so strong she feared she couldn't control it. She would often journal and some pages were quite ragged and torn from the scribbles that vented the anger when there were no words. Occasionally a co-resident would join her and together they would sit looking out the window understanding each other's pain. But she was not like some of the others who had mental illnesses and it would cause the weekend houseparents to ask what she's doing in that place.

They set up a support group for her and found a place for her to live. The support group went well but after 2 months she was told to move because of misunderstandings. So the support group took on the responsibility of finding her a new place to live. She also got a job at a local grocery  store. She tried to make the best of the living situation but it finally came to the place that each went their way and she just lived there but didn't share much of her life or happenings with the couple she now lived with. Her job was okay but the one owner made it miserable for everyone because she just couldn't seem to be pleased with anything sometimes.

About 3 yrs later she had a day off so she decided to go shopping with a friend. The friend suggested stopping in at a certain grocery store to which she agreed. While shopping, she was looking at the raw meat prices as she would cut the steaks etc. at her job and was just comparing prices.

The meat manager asked if she needed anything and so she explained what she was doing. He then suggested that if she was looking for another job they could use her and explained how bad language was not allowed and a few other things that appealed to her. She walked out of the store that day with an application and a week later she gave her 2 weeks notice at her job after accepting the job at the interview. She had no idea that at this job she would make some very huge, life-changing choices.

Part 6

On March 7, 2016 she biked the 6 miles to show up for her first day at work in the deli. For a few months she worked in the deli but did not like it. She felt stuck in one place. At the same time she had also been going to a counselor an hour away.

One day she got a phone call saying that her driver could not take her and she was in tears because she was learning to trust and this was important to her. On top of it the deli manager also said that she will probably be asked to stay and work till 8 and she didn't want to because she was scared to bike home in the dark. By then she was warming up to her new employer's wife and her kind ways so she tried to contain her tears and went over to the lady and asked if she had to stay till 8. The lady said no, he wasn't supposed to say anything and asked the girl if she was okay because she could see that something was troubling her.

She replied that yes, she just found out that she wouldn't be able to go to her counselor that day and offered that she could stay if she was needed. Her offer was accepted and before she walked away the lady told her that if she ever wanted to talk she was available. Later that day they found a quiet place and she told the kind lady some of her past and her struggles and before she went back to work the lady opened her arms to give her a hug. As the girl rested her head against the chest of the lady in a close embrace for a few seconds, she realized that this was exactly what she had always longed for from her mom. Her own mom was always too busy to lend a listening ear and had so much pain in her own heart that she used work to drown the pain and thus could not be there emotionally for her children or have a close relationship with them. And so started a new relationship of learning to trust on a deeper level.

In the meantime one day she came back to the warehouse in time to see the freezer girl come out of the cooler with her employer. The freezer girl was so excited with all she had gotten done and had wanted to show him how well she had cleaned up the freezer. As they closed the door he turned around and gave the freezer girl a high five. As the girl pondered this incident she realized that deep in her heart she feared all men but she saw no reason why she couldn't trust this man. He gave her no reason to fear him. But still the fear was so deep that there were times when he came walking in her direction that she nearly panicked. So as her trust grew with the kind lady she asked her one day how she could overcome this fear of the kind lady's husband. The lady said that her husband considers it proper to greet everyone with a good morning when they see each other in the morning and so suggested that maybe she could come to the office and say good morning to him. It looked terrifying but she wanted to overcome the fear so she decided to try it.

Part 7

The next morning as soon as she had a break from her work in the deli she slipped up front to the office. She had to walk through the kind lady's office to get to her husband's office and as she peered through the doorway trying to muster up enough courage she saw the kind lady standing by her husband's desk facing him while he was reclined in his office chair with his feet propped on the desk. She could tell that the lady knew she was there and so it gave her courage and she stuck her head far enough in to see the man's face, said "Good morning" and nearly ran out the door.

Before she went back to work she stopped at the water fountain for a drink in an effort to calm herself because she was almost shaking in her shoes, hardly believing that she had actually done it. As she looked up, she saw the kind lady coming towards her with a smile on her face. The lady said "That was cute!" and gave her a high five.

Later when she had a chance and was calmed down, she asked the kind lady what her husband did after she said good morning. The lady replied that he asked who it was. When she told him, his reply was "But I didn't get to say good morning to her." When the girl heard this it surprised her and she thought,"He really wanted to say good morning to ME?!" And so began another step in the journey of learning to trust a man who would soon become a fatherly figure in her life.

Since she did not like the deli she requested to be moved to the sales floor to stock. Her request was accepted and as she learned the procedure she grew to love her job because she liked filling and organizing the shelves.

As winter drew closer she realized that biking 12+ miles each day besides working a full day was wearing her out so she decided to look for a place closer to work. Because of all her painful experiences of living with others she decided she wants to live by herself. God provided a place she could afford that was only a mile from work.

As she settled in and did not have to fear what others thought in the household, God took the opportunity to bring up all the spiritual and religious questions that had plagued her for years. As her relationship grew in trust with her employer and his wife, she ventured out and began to ask them questions. One of the first questions she asked was about fasting. She wanted to understand it. As she learned that she can fast for struggles in her life and that it is a way to humble herself before God and show Him that she really wanted God to work in a situation, one day she asked if it is okay to fast for God to work in someone else's life. The answer was yes and so she began to fast for God to work in her family's dysfunctional situation. In one of the next conversations she was instructed to be ready because she might be the sacrifice it takes for God to work in her family.

With that in mind she began asking God to prepare her heart for whatever it might take. During the next few weeks the many questions she had suppressed for so long began to surface in her mind rapidly. Since she had several times tried to get answers from people and none satisfied her, she turned to the Lord and asked Him to show her the answers to her questions as she studied His Word. Many an evening was spent studying the Scriptures seeking answers with the help of her Strong's Concordance to help understand the meaning of the original Greek words. God saw her seeking, sincere heart and gave her the answers she was seeking for.

Soon she realized that she no longer agreed with the guidelines of her church and longed for a church that did as the Bible said. With that quest in mind she brought up the situation to the kind lady and discovered that it gives a type of church called Holiness Pentecostal and it was exactly what she knew she wanted. As she considered the situation she wrote down the reasons why she didn't want to leave her church, why she felt like she needed to, and what would change if she did. God used the opportunity to show her that she had a choice to make: she could stay a member of that church and please her parents or she could leave that church and obey God by what He had revealed to her through His Word. Faced with the immensity of the decision she faced, she took the paper with her list and gave it to her employer asking him if he and his wife would pray that she would make the right decision. To her surprise later that day he called her to his office and talked to her about each thing on her list and then prayed for her before letting her go. It meant much to her knowing that she had their support. She chose to follow God and God was ready to take her to another level.

Part 8

A month or 2 after she went to a small church that was having a fellowship meeting and her employer was to preach. She did not know what to expect and having only been in that church one time it was all still new to her. After the message there was an altar service and people went up to be prayed for. She watched as her employer, now in the role of a preacher of the Word, prayed for people. She tried to understand what he was saying and the people around him but she was puzzled because she could not understand. When the service was almost over a man in the back spoke out in a very loud voice and she watched as everyone got very quiet and bowed their heads. She was puzzled.

On the way home her coworker who had taken her along said that she doesn't really believe in speaking in tongues. A light went on in the girl's mind."Is that what they were doing?" she asked. The answer was yes and with that in mind she was determined to ask her employer the next day about it.

The next day she approached him in a quiet place and asked him if they were really speaking in tongues the night before. "I was expecting you to ask me," he replied and then proceeded to explain what all was going on the evening before and the Scriptures for it while in her heart began to grow the desire to also be filled with the Holy Ghost. From then on she began to ask God to baptize her with the Holy Spirit.

When she had made her decision she told her mom. Her mom was in shock and began to cry and then requested when the girl comes home to visit she would still wear her Mennonite clothes. The girl found it hard to because it reminded her of all the bondage she left behind but she remembered the Scripture that says "Honor thy father and mother"...

Her sister sent her a letter telling her why she shouldn't leave the church and how disappointed they are in her. Another friend who had been with her through some of the hardest times of her life also sent her a letter scolding her for her choice and telling her to change her mind. As she read the biting words in the letter, a joy that she had never felt before rose in her heart and filled her eyes with tears because she knew that she had made the right choice. But one day to her surprise one of her younger sisters called her, saying, "I want to hear your side of the story." God took the opportunity to cause friendship to blossom even deeper between her and most of her younger siblings because before everyone just looked out for themselves and no one was close to each other. They looked up to her and asked for advice and had many questions that she tried to answer best she knew how and now thanks God for the privilege of being the oldest sister.

After she made her decision public, her style of dress changed and one day her chiropractor came up to her at work and told her that he felt like God wanted him to give her the extra car that he and his wife had. She gratefully accepted because she had been wondering what to do about a car because she wanted to go to church. To her, learning to drive was terrifying so she didn't do much about it. The study guide just lay aside gathering dust till one morning on the way to work, it dawned on her that God had given her a car and was waiting for her to accept it! With that in mind she was determined to brave the step and learn to drive. It was frightening to the girl but she soon learned how and with great excitement she went on Nov. 29, 2017 to the DMV center to take her driving test. The instructor noticed and mentioned that she had a smile on her face to which she replied that she was just so excited. She passed and with great excitement she made plans to attend church the next Sunday 1.5 hours away.

Part 9

About 6 months later a neighboring church(in the same town of the church she was attending) had a youth weekend for the first time and being so hungry for church and God she went.

The first night the preacher preached on surrendering everything to God. As she searched her heart for anything she might not have surrendered to God the only thing she could think of was church. The church she was going to was the only one she really knew of and after praying about it and surrendering it to God, there were a few very sad days realizing that God had another place for her and that meant leaving behind the church family she knew. So for the next month or 2 she spent the week asking God where He wanted her to go and then would go to the church she felt led to go, keeping an eye out for events at churches she hadn't yet been to.

One Monday night in the middle of June she went to a church 3 hours away and when she walked in late with the singing already started she felt like she was already known and like she had come home even though the only person she slightly knew was the pastor's wife. Only God can make a person feel like that.

A few months later the landlord's cat who always came over for milk would walk in front of her so that she often almost tripped over the cat and for some reason that week it just made her so angry.

Towards the end of that week she set up an account on Facebook and a girl she had once met posted pictures of her animals. As she looked at the pictures, flashbacks started to overwhelm her of how she had often watched her dad beat the animals and how deep down she had actually feared for her life. With the memories fresh in her mind along with all the pain and fear she hardly slept that night. She was determined to ask the kind lady to pray for her when she had a chance because she wanted to be healed of the memories and didn't want them to control her present and future.

The lady prayed for her and they went their ways but the girl, deep down in her heart told God that she never heard of anyone getting healed like this before but she believes that He is able. As she went about her work about half an hour later she started feeling better and throughout the day she just kept feeling better and better. She was so excited because she knew it was not the coffee she drank that morning because this was a different feeling. It was not till 9:00 that evening that she realized she didn't even feel tired, which was amazing because she had barely slept the night before. The painful memories and fears have not bothered from that day to this because God touched her.

Towards the fall one Saturday evening she was on the way to church when she received a text from the kind lady saying that her husband was planning to start a Bible study on Wednesday nights and maybe eventually a church. She was so excited because it was an answer to prayer. She did all she could to support the Bible study, posting fliers and inviting people. She wanted it to work and not be a failure. She yearned for a church that taught holiness and was filled with the Holy Spirit in her area so bad. But it was not to be. After she poured her heart into it for several months she found out that the doors were being closed. Her dreams were shattered, her heart broken, and her dreams were crushed.

She had been warned that it might not last but in her mind she couldn't understand how a Bible study was supposed to succeed if her heart and effort wasn't poured into it. It left her with many haunting questions and many tears.

One thing that did happen during those Bible studies was that she had been sick with some unknown illness for almost 2 weeks and felt the need to be prayed for. It had drained her energy and left her feeling exhausted so that she felt like even her lungs were shutting down. That day 2 weeks after she first felt the illness coming on she asked to be prayed for at the Bible study that evening. Throughout the day she kept feeling worse and worse as now her throat had started hurting and by evening it was hard to swallow.

When she got to the Bible study that evening they told her they had forgotten the oil so they will just pray the prayer of faith. Before getting started with the study he asked her to come up front along with his wife and asked the congregation to stand and stretch their hands towards the front and pray for her. Afterwards the study started and the girl swallowed. Yes it still hurt, but instead of focusing on the pain and exhaustion she tried to focus on the message instead. About 5 minutes later she happened to swallow and all of a sudden she realized that it no longer hurt. Needless to say, she didn't get much out of the rest of the service. She just kept wondering about the change she felt in her body. The pain was gone and so was the weird exhaustion. She still felt tired and not wanting to say she's been healed for fear it wasn't real, she told nobody but decided to wait to see how she feels after a good night's rest. The next morning she knew she was healed and could not keep it quiet. God has a gentle touch.

Part 10

She tried to go on despite feeling like she had nothing left to live for after the Bible study ended. She wanted to do something for God and it seemed like the only outlet she knew of was gone. She did the best she knew how at the church she was attending but because of the distance she couldn't be there for most of the activities and services. What was left to live for?

On New Year's Eve her church was having watchnight service. Part way through the service the Presence of the Lord was so rich but the girl was struggling so she knelt and cried out to God. A few minutes later her pastor asked if she could stand up, so she did. With him was one of the preachers who had been invited to preach at the service and as the girl looked into their faces wondering what was about to happen, he spoke and said,"This afternoon when I was praying your face came to mind and God told me that He saw when you wondered in your heart whether this was all there was to life and God told me to tell you that there's so much more!" She lifted her hands and praised the Lord.

She had been asking God every day for almost 2 years to fill her with the Holy Ghost. One Sunday during a good service she felt like God refreshed her burden to pray more for her family. Because she lived so far away and didn't often get to see them she often forgot how it was at home and about her younger siblings growing up in that environment.

    The next day, on March 25, 2019, she went to her secret place to pray on her lunch break; which had developed as a habit several months before when she felt like God was calling her to pray more and so she had chosen to give up her lunch break for prayer. As she sought God to save her family she felt God's presence like she often did before but this time was a little different. She was trying to obey with all her heart what she felt like God had impressed upon her the evening before but for some reason she could only pray for so long till she couldn't control her mouth anymore. It was a little scary because she had never felt this before so she tried to keep on praying, stopping when she could no longer control her mouth but she felt something happening inside her heart. She had never seen or heard anyone get baptized with the Holy Ghost so she didn't think she got filled. She soon had to go back to work but all afternoon she pondered how her jaw still had a funny feeling and how something had changed on the inside. From then on whenever she was in a church service and the presence of God was strong, her lips would tremble and she couldn't hardly control her tongue. She didn't understand it at all even though she knew something had happened on that day.

    About a month or so later they were having an good service at church and God was touching folks. She was praying for a girl and since she didn't think she was yet filled with the Spirit she asked the Lord if He wouldn't fill her while He's helping all these other people too. Instead of focusing on what was happening to her mouth she focused on trying to pray for the other girl beside her. As she was trying to pray she all of a sudden realized that her tongue was making a noise she could not make though she had tried many times before. As soon as she became aware of what was happening it stopped but not before she knew what had happened. She told nobody but pondered it in her heart until the next Sunday when she told her pastor and his wife who greatly rejoiced. As church started her pastor who had lately been talking about good news asked the congregation if they wanted more good news. He then asked her to come up front and gave her the mic. All she could say was,"I got filled with the Holy Ghost and I'm so happy."

Part 11

One day a few months later the girl got a letter along with her check stub. A letter meant something was in the air so she went to the bathroom where she'd have privacy to read it. Because of her relationship with her employer and his wife she was extra sensitive to what the letters contained. They had been like parents to her and she couldn't imagine life without them if they ever moved away. She opened the letter but was not prepared for what it contained. It brought news that the store was in the process of being sold. She was so shocked that she had no words, not even a tear. She had thought about it and tried to imagine what it would be like but never dreamed it would actually be real.

The next several days were a blur wrapped in shock but through it all she felt something inside of her that she had never felt before, an anchor that kept her stable and able to work and function despite the shock. It was true what God had said was that He would pour out His Spirit on His children and along with the Spirit they would also receive a power they didn't have before.

The next week the kind lady came around the corner and wrapped her arms around the girl and murmured "I know you've been quiet lately but don't cry. I'm still here. You can still talk to me. I love you." It broke the bubble of shock and as soon as possible she went to the restroom and wept. The love she felt in that hug and the kind words brought peace to her troubled soul. As time went on and the news became reality, she spent much time seeking the Lord because she didn't know how she would survive. She didn't talk much with her employer and his wife but spent her time praying and crying to God. The Holy Spirit became her constant companion and she would often be quietly speaking in tongues as she went about her work. She tried to adjust to the changes as the new owner took over. After the store was sold, her former employer and wife were now training the new owners.

A few weeks later her former employer called her into the office. She didn't know what to expect but was not prepared for the words she would hear. She had no idea how to deal with the great loss she was facing and so didn't talk much to those around her. She had trusted them to the point that they could have almost brainwashed her in some ways. She tried to adjust the best she knew how.

In the office that day her salvation was questioned and she was told to go home and make sure that she really was saved. She was told that if she wants friends she must stop isolating herself. She had been warned before that she should not see them as parents and it had been confusing to her because to her they weren't her parents but they were filling the place her parents never had and she didn't know what to do to change it and it didn't help that her employer and his wife felt that they were her "spiritual guides". When asked if she had any questions she asked some of the questions that had puzzled her for a long time but they had no answers. She asked if people can have the Holy Ghost if they're not saved. The answer was no. Finally it just looked to her as though all her effort and struggle in trying to learn how to have proper relationships was worth nothing. To her everything in the relationship that she had worked so hard and longed for was crumbled to the ground. Shattered. Crushed. Broken. She lifted her arm to cover her face and let the tears flow. She felt the Holy Ghost and knew she wasn't alone though she felt like a beaten puppy cowering in a corner. After gaining control and a bit more talk he was ending the time together by praying for her but before he could finish the girl could no longer control the sobs that welled up out of her broken heart. She burst into sobs, not caring anymore who heard. Within a minute the Holy Ghost took over and the sobs turned into tongues only God could understand.

After a few minutes he told her that they need to move on because they are holding up other people from their work. So she was dismissed to go home after being in the office for 3 hrs. She went home and spent an evening full of misery and confusion. She wanted to do as he said but was so confused. She no longer knew what to believe. She wondered if all the times she had felt God's Presence or felt God speaking to her heart was all in vain. Was all the effort she had put into seeking for hope and answers and God, was all in vain and that she had actually been deceived? Devastating. But God saw it all.

The next Sunday morning her pastor's wife tried to comfort her. But the best place she found comfort was in pouring out her broken heart at the altar to the God who knew all about it. As time went on, she began to see things in a different light and wondered why she didn't see some things before but she tried to forgive because she didn't want bitterness to ruin her testimony for the Lord.

Part 12

In the middle of this huge change she found out that she needed to move. She was overwhelmed but she started searching for another place. All the doors closed in the area she wanted to move to so she got scared and thought that perhaps she's looking in the wrong direction. She kept asking God to open the door for her because she wanted to be in the center of His will.

After about 2 weeks of searching she connected with a lady that wanted her to rent their mobile home. When the girl stated the price of rent she could afford paying the lady took her up on it even though they had been getting more from the former renters. They badly wanted to accept the offer because they wanted someone they could trust around their children. They decided on an evening for the girl to come look at the place. It was a bit smaller than she was used to but the setting was exactly what she wanted. The mobile home was in the process of being remodeled and to the girl it was as though she would have a new house because the place she was living in was a mobile home that was at least 50 years old and was not very tight at all when it came to cold windy days. It all seemed to be too good to be true and she didn't know what to think so she texted her pastor's wife who in turn told her to ask God to give her peace about it if that's where He wanted her. So she asked God to give her peace about it and help her to know His will.

She woke up about an hour earlier than usual the next morning and instantly became aware that it felt like God was standing there holding out this blessing of a new and better place He wanted to give her and wondering how long it will take till she accepts this blessing. Right away she knew that this was God's will and with all doubts gone she moved ahead to accept all God wanted to give her in this new place. She had a desire for ministry and did everything she could come up with in her creative imagination to make it a comfortable, inviting, restful place. Her vision was to provide a place for any lady that needs a place to just get away from daily life, to have time to be alone with God, or any other reason some may have. She knows she doesn't have all the answers but if she can only provide a place apart for some troubled soul to find rest and to grow spiritually, her heart is full. Just like Jesus said to His disciples at the well after the Samaritan woman went her way after her conversation with Him,"I have meat to eat that you know not of."

As time went on she thought she seemed to be adjusting well to the changes till one day after talking to the kind lady, the new owner's wife pulled her aside and told her that she should take time off her paycheck for talking so long.She was puzzled and couldn't understand why she is being punished because never before did she get in trouble for talking. She suggested giving up her lunch break but the new lady said she should take a break. She didn't know what to say, so she asked, "What do you want me to do?" So the agreement was made that she would take an hour off her hours for the week. She couldn't believe she was hearing right but agreed because she didn't want to argue. She was very disappointed in the new owners. She expected them to treat the employees as Christians should. But instead things grew worse. Her manager, who was the best one she ever had, was demoted to the warehouse for unknown reasons. In her place was a new manager who was very rude and mean to the employees. She only lasted a few weeks. Not long after the new manager was fired, her former manager was told that she's hostile, causing drama and problems, and on Monday they will have a meeting. Depending how the meeting goes she will be fired. So everyone came to work dreading what the day holds because nobody wanted to see her fired and no one could understand the accusations. The girl heard her former manager say that if she got fired she would tell the new owners how things really stood saying she might just leave in a police car because she didn't know how she would react. The girl saw a need for God to move and texted several people asking them to pray that God would intervene. Mid-morning the former manager got a text saying that the manager meeting would be the next day. She just said, "I guess that's good."

Later in the afternoon the girl came back to the warehouse and one of the others told her that the former manager was now asked if she would go for produce so that the produce manager could spend more time with his people. She couldn't believe what she was hearing. Her former manager just said, "It makes me feel like I hallucinated on Saturday." It was traumatizing to the girl and all week she was not herself.

The girl was having a hard time relaxing at work and so she thought she would look for another job but God told her to wait through a message that was interpreted at church. She kept doing the best she knew how because she didn't know just how long she'd have to wait till God would release her from waiting. About a week later she was getting ready for work and decided to read over the message God had given her that she had written down so she could read it later. There had been a phrase that just didn't seem to fit right with the rest of the message and as she read over it again that morning it just popped out at her like God was trying to tell her something. It was about seeking and looking to God. So she started asking God for a confirmation and her pastor's wife also told her that she shouldn't do anything till she knows for sure. Monday evening she asked God again for a confirmation and every time she had asked before she felt God very strongly and this time she felt God so strongly that it scared her so she texted her pastor's wife. Her pastor's wife texted back saying Don't be afraid, but go and start looking for another job.

Part 13

The next day was her day off. She went to one place but just wasn't sure about it because she didn't want to be a cashier. She left without saying anything. She applied at 3 other stores and then as she was at the fourth place filling out an application her phone rang. It was the manager at the third place that she had applied to, wondering if she could come for an interview sometime. So she went back as soon as she was done filling out the application and he said he would start her out at $9 an hour but she said she couldn't do it at that because of her rent and utilities. He also wanted her to be a cashier which she refused. So then he mentioned that his dad might need someone to clean for him and that he owns the first place she'd stopped at that morning. He wrote down the name and phone number and she stuck it in her purse.

She had done cleaning before and was not too thrilled about getting back into it. The next evening one of her friends texted her saying that there is an Amish lady that is looking for a driver/cleaner for her cleaning business. She added the info to the paper that the man had given her with his dad's phone number and stuck it to the side. She wasn't too interested. That weekend she applied at another job that was closer than all the prior ones that she had applied at. She really hoped to get this job. But nobody was calling her about her applications and she started wondering if perhaps those weren't the places God wanted her. So she kept praying about it and one morning she woke extra early and couldn't get the cleaning jobs out of her mind. Before she left for work she left a message for the Amish lady.

That evening the Amish lady called her back and in the course of conversation she said she only had part time work. The girl said she would call the other place and maybe it would be possible to mesh the 2 jobs together. The next day on her day off the girl called the other place and he said he needed someone to work in the store, the very store that she had stopped in at the beginning. She agreed and went over later in the afternoon. He explained to her how he likes his store to look neat and clean which is something she loves to do. He asked if she minds cutting fabric to which she replied it was okay. She doesn't mind it. She found herself relaxing as he showed her around a little bit and asked more questions. The thing she was the most worried about was being a cashier and being paid enough so she can meet her rent and utility payments. She assumed that it mustn't be a big deal to not be a cashier because he didn't mention it and he agreed to pay her at least the same amount as she was getting at her old job. He also asked if she minds working outside that his wife might need help with cleaning and shrubbery through the summer to which she said she wouldn't mind. In the end she saw nothing to keep her from taking the job and so when he asked she accepted the position. As she walked to her car after the interview, the tears flowed. She struggled to grasp what had just happened... She had a new job!

She gave her quitting notice the next day at work and the next week and half at her old job was bittersweet. She was glad to move on from this now stressful job yet her place of work for the past 4 years held many memories. She couldn't hardly grasp that she was actually starting a new job but she felt like that was the direction God wanted her to go and she wanted to be where God wants her and so begins a new chapter in her life.

Part 14

The pandemic came by only 2 months later resulting in the worldwide shutdown except essential workers resulting in her being laid off for 4 weeks, putting her in a unique spot. Not enough money to even pay rent; resulting from spending most of her savings in buying for her new house she moved to half a year ago plus at her new job she worked less hours than her former job and therefore resulted in less income. She didn't know how she would make ends meet but wanted to trust the Lord to meet her needs. At the counsel of a pastor friend she applied for unemployment. In the waiting time, she was struggling to trust the Lord one day and when she fetched the mail there was a card from her secret sister at church and inside the card was a $50 Walmart gift card. She also was approved for unemployment and therefore it brought her through the shutdown until she could go back to work. Through it all the question niggled at the back of her mind "God, where's the so much more You have promised me?"

A few months later she got an invitation from her sister-in-law for a baby shower. She felt in her heart that it was time to go visit her family again, so she made plans to surprise them all. Since the shutdown money wasn't flowing as freely as before and since she didn't like to go empty handed, she found a few things here and there but she always liked to meet the needs that she knew of and could. There were things that her sister-in-law needed, so she spent time sewing necessary things and having so much fun doing it.

A few weeks later the timing belt broke on her '94 Camry and since it would cost over $500 to fix it and she was already a bit scared to drive the 3 hours to church every weekend because there were things she knew would only be a matter of time before it would need to be fixed. She decided to sell it after praying about it because she really wanted the Lord to lead the way before her in such a way that she would be able to glorify Him through her testimony. So she called the people who had put ads for junk cars in the newspaper but the highest anyone would go was $150. She felt that was too low and so in asking her pastor found that it was worth around $200. That weekend her church was shut down because of people sick with the virus. Someone from church had contacted her and said they felt led to give her $1,000 toward a new car, so she went to get it as she didn't know how soon she would need it. The next week her landlady told her of an app where a lot of Mennonite people use to buy and sell among their own, so she downloaded it and advertised the car for $500. A few people inquired but nobody followed through. So the next week she posted again. A day or two later her landlady told her she might need to reduce the price. By then she had gotten a call from her mechanic asking how she's making out because the car was sitting in his way and he couldn't budge it. So she reposted it for $400 and got a number of inquiries. The first person wanting to check it out tried to change the day till later in the week but she replied that she had 2-3 others waiting for him to decide whereupon he decided to come look at it that night yet. He brought his uncle with him to help him check it out but after looking over the whole thing he looked at her and said,"So the price is $400?" which she affirmed. He then asked if she would take $350 to which she agreed and decided to meet at the notary the next evening.

The next day they found out the notary closes early due to the next day being a holiday so they found another one. When she walked into the notary's office he handed her $360 and wouldn't take change. The rest of the transaction was taken care of and they both walked out happy; she because the car was finally sold and he was so excited because he now had a vehicle that was better on gas than his truck that he drove half an hour to and from work each day.

The girl now spent a lot of time looking online at neighboring car dealers to see if she couldn't find something in her price range. One of her co-workers and her husband took her under their wing and took her to a car dealer they trusted and told him what she was looking for and he would see if he could find something for her. In the coming days though all he could find was above her price range. Finally she found a second choice for $7,000 car half an hour away. She took it to her mechanic to check it out for her, which he did, but suggested that she should check Craigslist as she might find something cheaper. She had felt peace about the car so decided to go for it. Her co-worker and husband went with her to do paperwork to put in an application for a loan.

Part 15

In the meantime a friend had posted on Instagram about a mission boot camp and she really wanted to go because she really wanted to learn more about being a missionary and doing something more for God. Because she felt this friend could be trusted and encouraged anyone considering it should go, she prayed about it until God gave her peace about going as she was apprehensive due to a former experience. That day someone slipped her $50. Later she posted about her trip to this camp and someone messaged her saying they felt led to send her a little money for the trip. The day before she left an envelope came in the mail containing $100 which was much more than she expected. She also sent in the registration in faith believing God would make a way because as of yet she didn't have a vehicle and she didn't know if she'd be allowed to drive the borrowed vehicle.

The loan she had applied for was also denied due to lack of credit unless she could pay $2,000 down and have a cosigner. A coworker gave her the needed $1,000 but wouldn't cosign. Not knowing what to do she decided to see what her bank would do. She applied and in the application process discovered that the car's value was only around $5,400 instead of the $7,000 the car dealer wanted. The next day she was discussing it with her co-worker who then got her husband to go back to the original car dealer she first had inquired at and to see if he wouldn't have something cheaper. He did and would need about $4,500 to put it on the road so she called the bank the next morning to cancel the first application and to reapply for the cheaper car. By then she had also found out that she may use the borrowed car for her trip which took a huge load off her shoulders.

She drove to church and spent the night there because it would be a little closer than driving directly from her house. The next morning she left before the service started for her goal was to drive the 7+ hours out through Ohio to Dryden Road Pentecostal Church to which she had been listening to for the past 4 years since she had left her old church. She wanted to meet these people whose voices and names she knew but wanted to be able to put faces to the names finally. She got there an hour before church and met up with the man and his wife who had reached out to her several years before in trying to help her find a church near enough to go to. She was surprised that even the pastor wanted to meet her. She was delighted with the warm welcome extended to her and fit right in and had church with the rest of them. Afterwards was given the option of staying at the church for the night or to come home with the man and his wife. She opted for the latter because she didn't have much of a social life due to losing most of her friends when leaving her former church and so decided to "live it up". They got pizza and invited all the neighbors from church over and had a great time fellow-shipping and of course she had lots of questions to answer as they all knew about this person who had been listening in on Mixlr and wanted to get to know her and her story. At one time she stopped to swallow and could've heard a pin drop as she realized that everyone was spellbound by her story which scared her a little because she wasn't expecting such interest in her story.

The next morning before she left the neighbor lady slipped money into her hand that she didn't get around to counting till Tuesday morning and found it was $100. She left around noon to go to the Southern Ohio Youth Campgrounds where the mission boot camp was being held. She got assigned to her bunk and from there headed to the first class. She thoroughly enjoyed the classes and learning new things and getting to know the people and for once she didn't feel alone in her desire to do more for the Lord because there were others who also wanted to work for the Lord. The theme was Beyond The Now, What's Next? The thing that spoke to her the most was how we need to stop reacting to the present and instead respond and go forward toward being creative in finding new ways to spread the Gospel when the old ways are no longer working. To reach the generation of today in a way that reaches them rather than sticking to the ways the generation before us may have used. Two classes spoke to her the most; the one which was about how to organize your life and get unnecessary things out of your life so that you might be more ready whenever God calls you to the mission field whether at home or abroad and the other one was about the gifts of the Spirit and an explanation of how each of the gifts work alone and together and was very informative. One day something happened with someone that she had a part in and she felt burdened to tell that person there is hope. A bit later one of the instructors came to her and asked her if she would testify in the service that night.

Of course she was nervous being in a new church and knowing she will be asked to testify before all these people she didn't know. She asked the Lord to take the anxiety away and to let His anointing be upon her when she testifies that she might deliver the burden He had laid on her heart. When her turn came and she took the mic in front of that crowd, she started speaking and the Lord took away her anxiety and anointed her so that she delivered her testimony with an ability that surpassed her own strength. A message of hope because there's a God who cares for each of us; the downtrodden, the hurting, the hopeless, the struggling, the sick, and anyone else that needs a Friend to help them do life.

Part 16

She left camp early as she had formerly planned to go visit her family and since it was around a 9 hour drive she left after breakfast. There was a friend in northeast Ohio that she hadn't seen for 5 years or more so met up with her for an hour at a coffee shop and had the opportunity to share with her friend about some of the things God had been doing in her life before driving the rest of the way to her sister's place where she planned to spend the night.

Before she had started on her trip she had felt hesitant to take along her Mennonite clothes that her mom had requested her to wear when she came home. She felt like she couldn't wear them but because she wanted to honor her parents she took them along. When she got to her sister's house she just felt that she couldn't wear those clothes and after discussing it with her sister she decided to pray about it some more. She just couldn't wear those clothes. So she just wore her regular clothes. The next morning after her sister had left to run errands she was sitting on the sofa writing out the message to go with the verse for the day, her book fell sideways and $100 slipped out. She sat stunned for a second and had no idea where it came from. God has ways to provide for His children when they put their trust in Him.

She managed to surprise each of her family members and enjoyed spending time with each of her siblings' families and at her parents' house. To her surprise her parents said nothing about her choice of clothes.

As she traveled back home a few days later she spent time processing all the things she had learned and experienced in the past week and a half. She was overwhelmed with the future rising up with possibilities before her beyond her wildest dreams.

When she got home she found that the loan she was waiting on was also declined. She didn't know what to do except to wait on the Lord to open the doors for her because she had no clue which direction to go. In the waiting she pondered on how God had made a way for her and not only had answered her question she had asked earlier in the year but had also answered another thing that had been puzzling her and she had forgotten about it besides providing for her financially, she wanted to testify of His goodness. Because she realized that she didn't deserve all the good things that the Lord was showering on her, she went to church to worship the Lord despite the needs she had.

The next evening she got a text from the lady who's car she had borrowed saying they will need the car back by Wednesday. So the girl explained how the loans kept being denied and didn't know what to do. The lady's husband called her and said that even though they could give her the $2,000 she still needed, it might be a wiser option to see if they could help her get a loan from their bank and so decided to try it on her lunch break the next day. The next day the girl didn't go to work because of the cold which would no doubt have riled up some nasty customers and therefore ended up going to the bank earlier. Two hours later she walked out with a loan. When she got home she called her insurance company and got that stuff straightened out and then called the car dealer asking if she could come over right away or if she had to have an appointment. He stuttered a bit in surprise and said he needed some time to clean it up first as it had just been sitting in the back row. So she went over at 6 pm and got everything taken care of and by 7 pm she walked out with a new car. When God decides to move, He can move fast!

One thing that was on her mind was maybe doing a Bible study and as she pondered the idea the question came to her Who Am I? And so she decided that it would be her next project to do for the Lord, for there are so many people who don't really know who they are or what their purpose in life is. They may not even feel as though they have a future and suicide seems to be the best way out. She understood all those feelings and desired to help people find their purpose and hope through the Bible for that is the Book that changed her life and the direction of her future.

Part 17

On Sept. 17, 2020 she traveled to Ohio once again for Missions Apprenticeship Program (MAP) Phase 2. She was still waiting for the final email and thinking that Friday night at 6 is when she needed to be at the location. She traveled out in time for Thursday evening service at Dryden Road Pentecostal Church. From there she went home with a lady she hadn't met before and was planning to help her around the house the next day till the time came to go to her destination.

In the early afternoon she decided to message the contact person just to make sure that she had the time right and get the final details. About half an hour later the lady got back to her saying that there was a misunderstanding, that the event isn't until the next weekend. You can imagine her shock! As she looked back over the details that she did have everything pointed to the next weekend and she had no clue how she even got the wrong dates in mind. So the only thing she knew to do was to ask the Lord to turn her mistake around and do something great with it.

First she messaged a guy at church asking if they had any place for her to stay at the church. He said sure that she shall just let him know when she's on the way. When she got there, he showed up with 2 other people from the church and gave her a tour of the small house connected to the church which they were giving her to stay in. They only warned her to not open the door when someone knocks as it could be someone asking for a handout (something she wasn't used to). They left and she brought her stuff in and started finding places for it when there was a knock at the door. She peeped out the window to find a car sitting out there and after a few minutes a voice rang out calling her by name so that she knew it wasn't just a stranger. She opened the door to find a lady from the church who handed her a $50 bill to go get groceries.

That evening or the next day she saw a Facebook post listing about 10 things that a food pantry could use that people may donate. She realized that she's actually in the area and it would be possible for her to bless them, only she didn't have any money to spare.

Sunday morning when she was telling the Lord about it for whatever reason $100 popped into her mind so she asked the Lord for $100 thinking that it really is a huge amount of money to ask for. After the morning service 2 people handed her money and when she got over to her house she counted it only to find $120! She thanked the Lord and planned the next day to go buy food to share.

Monday night found her at the food pantry and she had the privilege of helping pack a few boxes and watch the process. It was just starting up so only a few people came and they all happened to come that night before it was even technically open. So everyone spent the rest of the time preparing and talking. When it was time to close up they started passing out food to take home that won't last till the next Monday. To her great surprise they loaded her up with a lot more food than she had brought. God just returned the blessing upon her own head which she hadn't expected at all. After all, earlier that day she had been worrying whether her groceries were going to last or not...

Tuesday and Wednesday she spent helping a friend with her in-home bakery. It was great to feel needed and that she was relieving a load on a mother's shoulders even though she wasn't very fast. It was also nice to be around people instead of just by herself.

Tuesday evening before church started she was chatting with the lady that sat behind her, one of the oldest members of the church. After service had started the lady tapped her on the shoulder and when she turned around the lady handed her a piece of paper and asked her to write her name on it so she could pray for her, which almost brought tears to her eyes.

Thursday she tried to pay the tuition for the weekend plans she had originally traveled out for but her credit card wouldn't go through and when she checked her bank account she realized that she didn't even have enough money to pay the bill. Then she started worrying how is she ever going to make it home. She took it to the Lord and tried not to worry about it.

Friday evening was to be the first session of Phase 2. It was about learning how to lead a prayer meeting. Everyone had the opportunity to take part in one and even though only one other person showed up the Presence of God was so rich in that place... Afterwards she was pulled aside by the pastor and was told that just before everyone arrived a lady with whom he had not spoken to in years found out this girl was to be there that night and God had told her to give her a certain amount of money. It was a $300 check! She almost cried. She had for the moment forgotten that she didn't know how she was going to make it home.

Saturday was a day full of classes till she felt like her head was about ready to explode. Sunday morning the group was back again and given an outline of what a church service looks like. Next everyone was dismissed for our assignments. She was assigned to share her testimony in the children's church. It was way out of her comfort zone as she'd never been in a children's church before nor had she ever shared her testimony on a child's level.

Most of the children were on a bus ministry route and not used to sitting still in a church service. After going over the rules and singing a song she was up next. She had been warned to expect acting out and talking but to just go on like she didn't hear. They all just sat spellbound!

In the evening she was back at Dryden Road for the evening service. It was bittersweet. Everyone was so kind and she didn't want to leave. God blessed her abundantly and had just been so good to her and it was with a heavy heart that she traveled home on Monday.

Part 18

After all that she experienced she wanted to move to Ohio. She thought she felt God calling her to move out there. She knew that before she could move she needed to pay off all her debt and so she trusted that God would make a way for her. As time went on that way was not made, but rather some other things started changing under the surface. God was still working, just in a different way and taking her in a different direction she never expected.

In the early spring of 2020 when the country was shut down for several weeks she realized she was only going to church for an emotional high and then she'd crash through the week because she lived 3 hours away and couldn't go to the mid-week service. Due to her history she already had an incredibly hard time knowing how to deal with her emotions and began to wonder if perhaps going to such a church was just compounding the struggle so she tried to be more careful and not be so easily swayed by emotions because after all the Bible says in Galatians 3:11 that no man is justified by the law in the sight of God, it is evident: for, The just shall live by faith.

Being interested in missions and wanting to do more for God she went to the mission events in OH that were mentioned earlier. While she was there she went to a church that had no holiness standards in dress and it put her so out of her comfort zone. Yet she felt the "presence of God" and saw God working and heard testimonies and she knew God was working there. When she came back and hoped to move to

Ohio to be with her friends and learn more about missions and to help in ministry and reaching people but she wasn't financially able.(She had left the Mennonite church some 3 yrs before and had lost basically all her friends and was currently traveling 3 hrs to a holiness Pentecostal church every weekend in another state.) Church authority did not approve of that liberal church and they did not want her to move out to that church. They said that they're worldly.

Another time she was told other people cannot get a hold of God like Holiness Pentecostals can because they live a holiness lifestyle. That got her attention and she couldn't agree. She had seen God work in that church. That would mean that most of the world's Christian population were not actually Christians and they were deceived. She did not see how the Bible would support that. The Bible says those that believe will be saved and then they are commanded to follow and obey God and His Word.

There had been an Indian couple coming to her church ever since she'd been going there and the lady wore jewelry as is common in her culture whether you're a Christian or not. One day on the subject of jewelry the girl was told that the Holiness people in other countries are loaded with jewelry but they don't have what we have because the Bible says jewelry is wrong. She couldn't agree with that either. What stood out to her was that her church is the right church and the rest just haven't had their eyes opened yet to Biblical truth. She hated what she saw in that. Pride. She didn't want pride in her life. There are many verses in the Bible that condemn pride.

During this time she came across this article: https://bereanholiness.com/can-women-wear-pants/ and she couldn't even open it to read it. It was too much of a change to even consider the idea that perhaps it was ok for women to wear ladies' pants in light of Scripture. She did read some of the other articles on the website and found them well written and very informative. She also came across this one:

https://bereanholiness.com/jewelry-on-trial/

Even though she also had a hard time looking at this one this may have been the first one she tried to digest. Even though she didn't read them for a while it made her think about what she called her convictions and whether they were actually her convictions or just men's teaching. Eventually she got the courage to read them and criticize them after she couldn't get them out of her mind but in the end it made her realize how foolish her arguments were (what she had been taught all her life).

In the middle of all this she was chatting with 2 ladies one evening and the one said, I haven't seen you run in quite awhile, to which the other agreed also(one of the men had been hinting at the same thing for quite a while). She was then told to be careful to not " lose her shout". It puzzled her and after she got over the shock of the statement the question in her mind was, where in the Bible is that? It is nowhere.

In the meantime I had gotten connected with one of the people behind bereanholiness.com

and got to hear of their research they had done to find out the origin of "shouting". I also did some research myself. Here is the most compiled article I found that not only confirmed my new friend's research but also had much more info than what my friend had shared with me:

https://www.understanding-ministries.com/docs/The%20Origins%20of%20Pentecostalism.pdf

Part 19

Through December 2020 she realized that she was not getting out of her debt hole like she was hoping and she began to wonder if perhaps it wasn't God's will for her to move to Ohio so over Christmas she fasted several days because she needed to know what direction God wanted her to go.

After that things seemed to break loose. It seemed as though her mind became more open to accept the things she had always been taught against. When church authorities found out that she had fasted, she was told that they had been begging God to hedge her in. (They had a "burden" for her area 3 hours away and believed she should stay where she is). That just kinda took the whole "wind out of her sails", especially when she was told that her desire to move to Ohio was just for herself because then she'd have a good church close by(not the liberal church mentioned earlier but one considered to be one of the best in the Holiness movement that is in the same area) and plenty of friends to hang out with, both things she didn't currently have. She didn't know what to think anymore.

How can she even know God's voice anymore with people projecting onto her their "burdens"?

She also began to realize how spiritually hungry she was. In her church the "Spirit was to lead" and therefore there kept being services where there was no preaching of the Word. She began to remember that the Bible says let all things be done decently and in order which was definitely not happening. She also realized how much she desired to be taught how to deal with the world in which she lived and how to let her light shine. There was no such teaching.

The focus was in having a "good service" which meant people speaking in tongues, shouting, being "slain in the spirit", running, and praying in the altars. All about experience. She didn't even remember the last time there had been a sermon preached. How was she supposed to know how to conduct herself in this present world if there's no instruction?

She knew she couldn't stay. She had to find another church. She was also hearing that there may be another shutdown and that the church may have to go underground soon and she realized from past experience(the shutdown last spring) that she would have nothing and no connection anywhere and so she was convinced that the wisest thing would be to look for a church in her own area and to get connected with Christians in the same area which is what she told church authority as her reason for leaving. She didn't mention the deeper issues that she knew God had been dealing with her about because she knew how church authority felt about it and she didn't want to leave on bad terms or damage more relationships than she had to. It did raise concerns in their eyes and maybe one day these things will come to the light but for now this is where it stands.

During this time she also listened to this video: https://www.youtube.com/watch?v=UsNesP8JnMY

and she heard about a nondenominational network of churches called Calvary Chapel so she decided to see if she could find one in her area and she did.

She started going and what she found was pure Biblical teaching and fellowship that she had been so hungry for. Not holiness standards. Not Mennonite standards. But she believed God had been dealing with her in preparing her for this step. She found that those people were just as much if not more Christians at heart as she was in holiness dress standards.

Soon after she started attending there was a women's event and even though she was scared to walk into a house full of strangers they just welcomed her right in. It turned into a very enjoyable evening. At the end all gathered together for a devotional time which was not something she was expecting. Then everyone split into small groups to share needs and pray for each other. It was a very good experience for her. Afterwards on the way home she was thinking about the whole event and she realized that she had not heard one word of bad language. She realized that they cared just as much if not more about each other than those in the holiness circles.

Her plans for that Sunday had been to go with a coworker to her church which she said is a little mission church in the midst of a nearby city but plans changed and so she ended up going to the Calvary Chapel church that she had been visiting on Wednesday nights. She found the service to be down to earth, simple, and very "filling". It was on Romans 2 and even though she didn't remember most of what was said she left feeling as though she had been fed spiritually till she couldn't hold any more. It was rich Biblical teaching that she'd never experienced before.

To this day she continues to attend this church, being discipled by some of the older ladies in the church as well as making new friends and being fed spiritually.

Though for the time being most of her ministry efforts have ceased due to working with a counselor and God leading her ever deeper into healing from the past, she looks forward to becoming a vessel that God can use in even more ways in the near future,

for God doesn't waste pain but rather He is more than able to redeem any pain experienced and use it for His glory...

And the story continues...

Now these Jews were more noble than those in Thessalonica;they received the word with all eagerness, examining the Scriptures daily to see if these things were so.
-Acts 17:11

Contact Info...

You can connect with me through my website at: www.lighthopetruth.com

If you are searching for some good solid Bible teachings, I recommend:
- -www.bereanholines.com
- -https://isgenesishistory.com
- -https://cc-chestersprings.com
- -https://rcc-newholland.com
- -http://thefuelproject.org
- -https://slowtowrite.com
- -https://drmsh.com
- -https://theremnantradio.com
- -https://thecultishshow.com
- -https://nakedbiblepodcast.com/episodes/
- -https://hischannel.com

I'm sure there's more good ones but these are some of the ones I have found that I thought were sound...

Contact Info... ~ 77

www.ingramcontent.com/pod-product-compliance
Lightning Source LLC
Chambersburg PA
CBHW042044290426

44109CB00001B/26